MW00914259

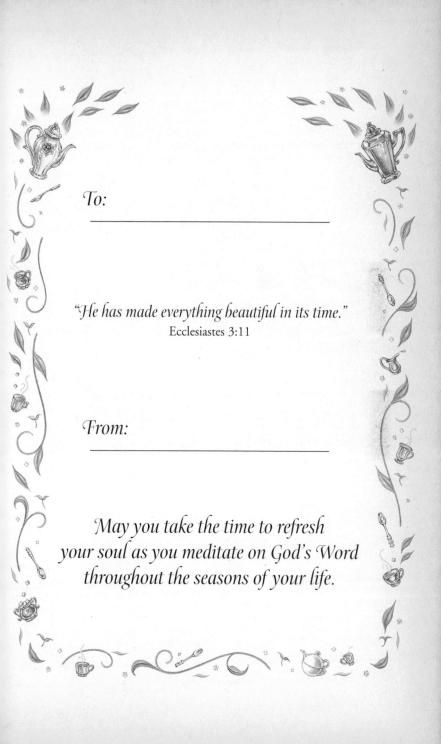

To:

_____

"He has made everything beautiful in its time."
Ecclesiastes 3:11

From:

_____

*May you take the time to refresh
your soul as you meditate on God's Word
throughout the seasons of your life.*

A Tea For All Seasons Journal
© 1997 The Zondervan Corporation
ISBN: 0-310-97300-7

Excerpts taken from *A Tea For All Seasons: Devotional Moments to Savor and Share*. Copyright © 1997 by Mary Pielenz Hampton

All Scripture quotations, unless otherwise noted, are taken from the *Holy Bible: New International Version*® (North American Edition). Copyright © 1973, 1978, 1984 by International Bible Society. Used by permission of Zondervan Publishing House. All rights reserved.

The "NIV" and "New International Version" trademarks are registered in the United States Patent and Trademark Office by International Bible Society.

All rights reserved. No part of this publication may be reproduced, stored in a retrieval system, or transmitted in any form or by any means—electronic, mechanical or photocopy, recording, or any other—except for brief quotations in printed reviews, without the prior permission of the publisher.

Published in association with the literary agency of Alive Communications, Inc., 1465 Kelly Johnson Blvd., #320, Colorado Springs, CO 80920.

Requests for information should be addressed to:

ZondervanPublishingHouse
Mail Drop B20
Grand Rapids, Michigan 49530
http://www.zondervan.com

Senior Editor: Joy Marple
Production Editor: Pat Matuszak
Project Editor: Leslie Berg Hoffman
Design: Cheryl VanAndel
Layout: Jody DeNeef

Printed in the United States of America
97 98 99 / RRD-C / 3 2 1

*T*here is a time for everything,
and a season for every activity under heaven.

Ecclesiastes 3:1

*D*o your moments seem to slip away with time?
How can you learn to appreciate the beauty of
each moment?

_____

_____

_____

_____

_____

_____

_____

_____

_____

_____

_____

_____

_____

_____

_____

_____

_____

_____

_____

_____

*H*e has made everything beautiful in its time. He has also set eternity in the hearts of men; yet they cannot fathom what God has done from beginning to end.

Ecclesiastes 3:11

*I*s your time on God's terms? Are you able to turn from your limitations of time and move beyond the scope of a sixty minute hour and twenty-four hour day?

_____

_____

_____

_____

_____

_____

_____

_____

_____

_____

_____

_____

_____

_____

_____

_____

_____

_____

_____

_____

Jesus Christ is the same yesterday and today and forever.
Hebrews 13:8

If Jesus is the "same yesterday and today and forever" does that mean with God there is only NOW? How might that change your perspective during the events of today?

_____

_____

_____

_____

_____

_____

_____

_____

_____

_____

_____

_____

_____

_____

_____

_____

_____

_____

_____

*T*he moon marks off the seasons,
and the sun knows when to go down.

Psalm 104:19

*W*hat is your favorite season? Are you able to
appreciate and thank God for the beauty of the
seasons' differences?

_____

_____

_____

_____

_____

_____

_____

_____

_____

_____

_____

_____

_____

_____

_____

_____

_____

_____

_____

And God said, "Let there be lights in the expanse of the sky to separate the day from the night, and let them serve as signs to mark seasons and days and years."

Genesis 1:14

Is there any passage of time to God as we define it by minutes and hours? Is it comforting to know that God is not limited by our definition of time?

_____

_____

_____

_____

_____

_____

_____

_____

_____

_____

_____

_____

_____

_____

_____

_____

_____

_____

I know that everything God does will endure forever;
nothing can be added to it and nothing taken from it.
God does it so that men will revere him.

Ecclesiastes 3:14

*D*o you realize there is always as much time to come
as there is time that has already been? Does this effect
your perception of the passage of time in your life?

_____

_____

_____

_____

_____

_____

_____

_____

_____

_____

_____

_____

_____

_____

_____

_____

_____

_____

_____

"*I* tell you the truth, this generation will certainly not pass away until all these things have happened. Heaven and earth will pass away, but my words will never pass away."

Luke 21:32–33

*D*o you take confidence in knowing that your life is not left to chance or random happenstance?

_____

_____

_____

_____

_____

_____

_____

_____

_____

_____

_____

_____

_____

_____

_____

_____

_____

_____

*T*he day is yours, and yours also the night; you established the sun and moon. It was you who set all the boundaries of the earth; you made both summer and winter.

Psalm 74:16–17

*T*ime was one of God's first creations. What methods have you created to keep track of time? Do you find it difficult to grasp a definition of time?

_____

_____

_____

_____

_____

_____

_____

_____

_____

_____

_____

_____

_____

_____

_____

_____

_____

_____

_____

_____

*A*s long as the earth endures, seedtime and harvest,
cold and heat, summer and winter, day and night
will never cease.

Genesis 8:22

*H*ave you been able to see the value in various seasons in
your life?

_____

_____

_____

_____

_____

_____

_____

_____

_____

_____

_____

_____

_____

_____

_____

_____

_____

_____

_____

Every good and perfect gift is from above, coming down from the Father of the heavenly lights, who does not change like shifting shadows.

James 1:17

Like a slowly brewing cup of tea, do you anticipate your time with the Lord? Do you look forward to your devotional time?

_____

_____

_____

_____

_____

_____

_____

_____

_____

_____

_____

_____

_____

_____

_____

_____

_____

_____

_____

_____

There is a time to plant and a time to uproot.
Ecclesiastes 3:2

Will you thank God today that the seasons in your life will never stand still? That each season plays a part in the creation of your character?

_____

_____

_____

_____

_____

_____

_____

_____

_____

_____

_____

_____

_____

_____

_____

_____

_____

_____

_____

*T*he one who received the seed that fell on
good soil is the man who hears the word and
understands it. He produces a crop, yielding
a hundred, sixty or thirty times what was sown.

Matthew 13:23

*H*ow can sharing the news of the kingdom of God be
compared to planting a garden?

_____

_____

_____

_____

_____

_____

_____

_____

_____

_____

_____

_____

_____

_____

_____

_____

_____

_____

_____

*Now faith is being sure of what
we hope for and certain of what we do not see.*

Hebrews 11:1

How strong is your faith when it comes to the health
and well-being of those you love? Do you trust God
to see them through the seasons of life?

_____

_____

_____

_____

_____

_____

_____

_____

_____

_____

_____

_____

_____

_____

_____

_____

_____

_____

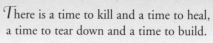

*T*here is a time to kill and a time to heal,
a time to tear down and a time to build.

Ecclesiastes 3:3

*S*itting down with a delicious cup of tea can be a very refreshing moment. Is your time with the Lord an experience of refreshment?

_____

_____

_____

_____

_____

_____

_____

_____

_____

_____

_____

_____

_____

_____

_____

_____

_____

_____

_____

_____

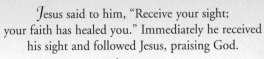

Jesus said to him, "Receive your sight;
your faith has healed you." Immediately he received
his sight and followed Jesus, praising God.

Luke 18:42–43

When you approach God for a "healing," do you
actually bring your deepest needs to Him? Or instead,
do you ask for what you think you need immediately?

_____

_____

_____

_____

_____

_____

_____

_____

_____

_____

_____

_____

_____

_____

_____

_____

_____

_____

_____

_____

Sow for yourselves righteousness, reap the fruit
of unfailing love, and break up your unplowed
ground; for it is time to seek the LORD, until he
comes and showers righteousness on you.

Hosea 10:12

*D*o you marvel at the beauty of the seasonal changes
of nature?

_____

_____

_____

_____

_____

_____

_____

_____

_____

_____

_____

_____

_____

_____

_____

_____

_____

_____

*F*or in the same way you judge others, you will be judged, and with the measure you use, it will be measured to you.

Matthew 7:2

*H*ave you ever been so concerned with another person's weaknesses that you try to look past your own shortcomings? What area(s) in your life does God want *you* to improve?

_____

_____

_____

_____

_____

_____

_____

_____

_____

_____

_____

_____

_____

_____

_____

_____

_____

_____

_____

*T*est me, O LORD, and try me, examine
my heart and my mind; for your love is ever
before me, and I walk continually in your truth.

Psalm 26:2–3

*W*ill you remember—today—to keep your eyes on
the One we should all strive to be most like and be
less concerned with what those around you are doing?

*F*ight the good fight of the faith. Take hold of the eternal
life to which you were called when you made your good
confession in the presence of many witnesses.

1 Timothy 6:12

*D*o you find it difficult to share God's love with a
stranger—with someone in the next seat on an
airplane, a clerk at a store, a lonely child in the
neighborhood? Why not take a deep breath—and
try it sometime?

_____

_____

_____

_____

_____

_____

_____

_____

_____

_____

_____

_____

_____

_____

_____

_____

_____

_____

_____

*H*e who loves a pure heart and whose speech
is gracious will have the king for his friend.

Proverbs 22:11

*W*hen asked a direct question, do you "tell it like it is?"
How can you make your speech more "gracious" in
such situations?

_____

_____

_____

_____

_____

_____

_____

_____

_____

_____

_____

_____

_____

_____

_____

_____

_____

_____

_____

I will bless them and the places surrounding
my hill. I will send down showers in season;
there will be showers of blessing.

Ezekiel 34:26

*A*re you a good steward with the blessings and riches He
has allowed you to possess? How do you show your
gratitude to God?

_____

_____

_____

_____

_____

_____

_____

_____

_____

_____

_____

_____

_____

_____

_____

_____

_____

_____

_____

Jesus looked toward heaven and prayed: "Father, the time has come. Glorify your Son, that your Son may glorify you. For you granted him authority over all people that he might give eternal life to all those you have given him."

John 17:1–2

*H*ow do you pray? On your knees? Sitting in a chair? Have you ever looked toward heaven when praying?

_____

_____

_____

_____

_____

_____

_____

_____

_____

_____

_____

_____

_____

_____

_____

_____

_____

_____

*T*here is a time to weep and a time
to laugh, a time to mourn and a time to dance.

Ecclesiastes 3:4

*D*o you think you'd have less cause for weeping and
regret if you focused on things that are pure and true?

_____

_____

_____

_____

_____

_____

_____

_____

_____

_____

_____

_____

_____

_____

_____

_____

_____

_____

*G*uard the good deposit that was entrusted to you—guard
it with the help of the Holy Spirit who lives in us.

2 Timothy 1:14

*W*ould it help revive your study time to remind yourself
that you are holding a personal message from God?

_____

_____

_____

_____

_____

_____

_____

_____

_____

_____

_____

_____

_____

_____

_____

_____

_____

_____

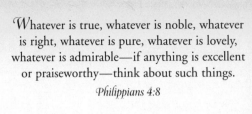

*W*hatever is true, whatever is noble, whatever
is right, whatever is pure, whatever is lovely,
whatever is admirable—if anything is excellent
or praiseworthy—think about such things.

Philippians 4:8

*D*o you sometimes give in to fear that you will not be
able to impact the world if you live at the heights
of holiness?

_____

_____

_____

_____

_____

_____

_____

_____

_____

_____

_____

_____

_____

_____

_____

_____

_____

_____

_____

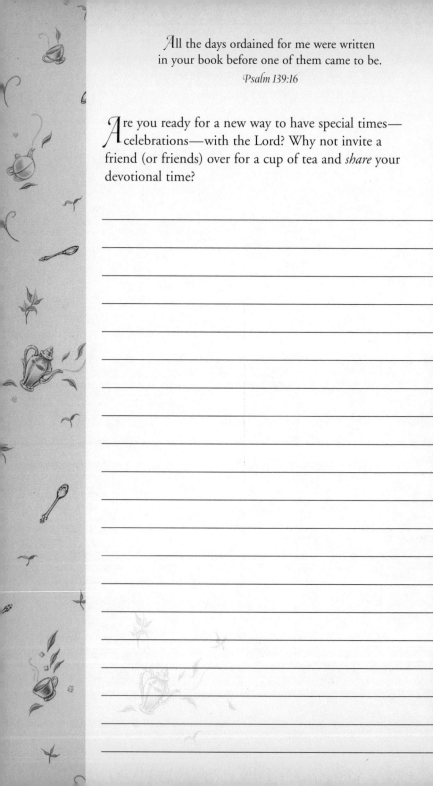

All the days ordained for me were written
in your book before one of them came to be.

Psalm 139:16

Are you ready for a new way to have special times—
celebrations—with the Lord? Why not invite a
friend (or friends) over for a cup of tea and *share* your
devotional time?

_____

_____

_____

_____

_____

_____

_____

_____

_____

_____

_____

_____

_____

_____

_____

_____

_____

_____

For the LORD is a God of justice.
Blessed are all who wait for him!

Isaiah 30:18

Although it can be painful or frustrating, do you believe that waiting for God's best is good?

_____

_____

_____

_____

_____

_____

_____

_____

_____

_____

_____

_____

_____

_____

_____

_____

_____

_____

_____

_____

*A*ll the believers were together and had
everything in common. Selling their possessions
and goods, they gave to anyone as he had need.

Acts 2:44–45

*A*lthough God may not physically partake of your
devotional time His presence can be very real. Can you
imagine a chair "reserved" for Him next to you?

_____

_____

_____

_____

_____

_____

_____

_____

_____

_____

_____

_____

_____

_____

_____

_____

_____

_____

There is a time to scatter stones
and a time to gather them.

Ecclesiastes 3:5a

Are you a "giving" person? Do you find it difficult to be free with your own possessions?

_____

_____

_____

_____

_____

_____

_____

_____

_____

_____

_____

_____

_____

_____

_____

_____

_____

_____

_____

_____

"*But* I tell you who hear me: Love your enemies,
do good to those who hate you, bless those who
curse you, pray for those who mistreat you."

Luke 6:27–28

*W*hen you read these verses, does anyone (or any group)
come to mind? Can you pray for that person (or group)
right now?

_____

_____

_____

_____

_____

_____

_____

_____

_____

_____

_____

_____

_____

_____

_____

_____

_____

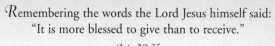

*R*emembering the words the Lord Jesus himself said:
"It is more blessed to give than to receive."

Acts 20:35

*W*hy do you think God encourages us to give to others?

_____

_____

_____

_____

_____

_____

_____

_____

_____

_____

_____

_____

_____

_____

_____

_____

_____

_____

_____

_____

*K*eep his decrees and commands, which I am giving
you today, so that it may go well with you and your
children after you and that you may live long in the
land the LORD your God gives you for all time.

Deuteronomy 4:40

*H*ow can you be an encouragement to others who
struggle through the waiting process?

_____

_____

_____

_____

_____

_____

_____

_____

_____

_____

_____

_____

_____

_____

_____

_____

_____

_____

*W*e give thanks to you, O God. . . . You say, "I choose the appointed time; it is I who judge uprightly. When the earth and all its people quake, it is I who hold its pillars firm."

Psalm 75:1–3

*D*o you look at work as a necessary evil? Is that how God views our given tasks?

_____

_____

_____

_____

_____

_____

_____

_____

_____

_____

_____

_____

_____

_____

_____

_____

_____

_____

_____

_____

*F*or even when we were with you, we gave you this rule:
"If a man will not work, he shall not eat."

2 Thessalonians 3:10

*H*ave you ever had to work at a job that seems "beneath your station" in order to support yourself or your family? Did you know God admires our willingness to "earn" our way?

_____

_____

_____

_____

_____

_____

_____

_____

_____

_____

_____

_____

_____

_____

_____

_____

_____

_____

_____

I know that there is nothing better for men than to be happy and do good while they live. That everyone may eat and drink, and find satisfaction in all his toil—this is the gift of God.

Ecclesiastes:3:12–13

*W*ould you get more satisfaction out of the chores that consume such a large percentage of your time if you looked at work as God's plan for our existence on this earth?

_____

_____

_____

_____

_____

_____

_____

_____

_____

_____

_____

_____

_____

_____

_____

_____

_____

_____

_____

He seldom reflects on the days of his life, because God keeps him occupied with gladness of heart.

Ecclesiastes 5:20

*O*ur culture focuses so much on retirement. Is retirement ever discussed in the Bible as a regular season of life for everyone?

_____

_____

_____

_____

_____

_____

_____

_____

_____

_____

_____

_____

_____

_____

_____

_____

_____

_____

_____

"*The* least of you will become a thousand,
the smallest a mighty nation. I am the Lord;
in its time I will do this swiftly."

Isaiah 60:22

*D*oes God expect everyone to have a paying job? If you
are not able to work (or have no need for a paying
job), how can you use your time to be a productive,
contributing member of society?

_____

_____

_____

_____

_____

_____

_____

_____

_____

_____

_____

_____

_____

_____

_____

_____

_____

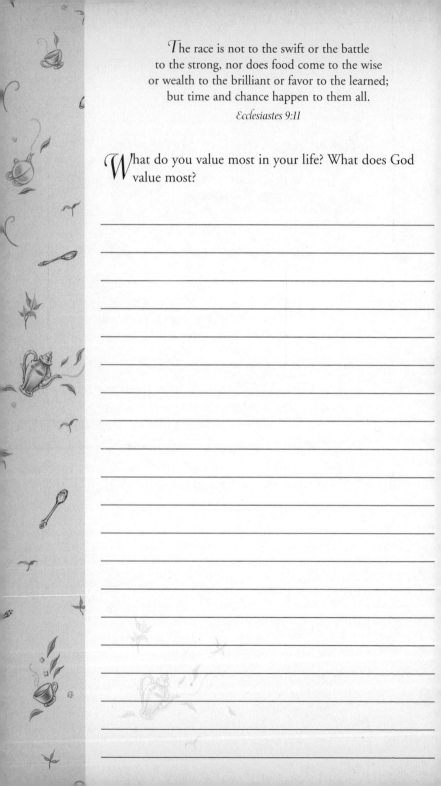

*T*he race is not to the swift or the battle
to the strong, nor does food come to the wise
or wealth to the brilliant or favor to the learned;
but time and chance happen to them all.

Ecclesiastes 9:11

*W*hat do you value most in your life? What does God
value most?

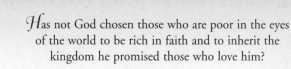

*H*as not God chosen those who are poor in the eyes
of the world to be rich in faith and to inherit the
kingdom he promised those who love him?

James 2:5

*D*o you treat the poor around you differently? Maybe
not—but how about people with different points of
view—political, theological, social?

_____

_____

_____

_____

_____

_____

_____

_____

_____

_____

_____

_____

_____

_____

_____

_____

_____

_____

_____

*T*here is neither Jew nor Greek, slave nor free, male nor female, for you are all one in Christ Jesus.

Galatians 3:28

*D*o you rejoice in God's great, unconditional acceptance of us? How can you show your gratitude?

_____

_____

_____

_____

_____

_____

_____

_____

_____

_____

_____

_____

_____

_____

_____

_____

_____

_____

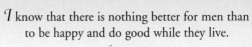

I know that there is nothing better for men than
to be happy and do good while they live.

Ecclesiastes 3:12

*H*ave you ever needed the help of others—for food
or clothing or shelter? Have you thanked God for
providing the ability to "earn" our way in some manner?

_____

_____

_____

_____

_____

_____

_____

_____

_____

_____

_____

_____

_____

_____

_____

_____

_____

_____

_____

*Y*ou show that you are a letter from Christ,
the result of our ministry, written not with ink but
with the Spirit of the living God, not on tablets
of stone but on tablets of human hearts.

2 Corinthians 3:3

*D*id you know that we are God's love letters to
the world?

_____

_____

_____

_____

_____

_____

_____

_____

_____

_____

_____

_____

_____

_____

_____

_____

_____

_____

There is a time to embrace and a time to refrain.
Ecclesiastes 3:5b

Do you follow Jesus' example of compassion toward the poor and "lowly?" Do you "embrace" others who are different than you?

_____

_____

_____

_____

_____

_____

_____

_____

_____

_____

_____

_____

_____

_____

_____

_____

_____

_____

_____

_____

*A*s believers in our glorious Lord
Jesus Christ, don't show favoritism.

James 2:1

*B*eyond feeding the poor or giving them your cast-off
clothing, do you treat them with the same respect and
humanity you offer anyone you view as your equal?

_____

_____

_____

_____

_____

_____

_____

_____

_____

_____

_____

_____

_____

_____

_____

_____

_____

_____

_____

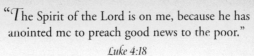

"*T*he Spirit of the Lord is on me, because he has anointed me to preach good news to the poor."

Luke 4:18

*D*o you show your gratitude for God's great, unconditional acceptance by extending acceptance to all those you encounter?

_____

_____

_____

_____

_____

_____

_____

_____

_____

_____

_____

_____

_____

_____

_____

_____

_____

_____

_____

_____

_____

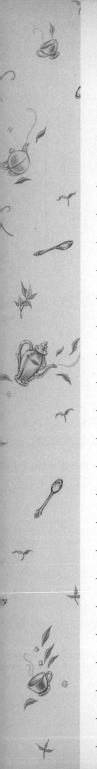

There is a time to search and a time to give up.
Ecclesiastes 3:6a

What is your treasure? Do you hold that treasure with an open hand that allows you to appreciate and enjoy it—but won't break your heart or cause great pain if it is lost somehow?

_____

_____

_____

_____

_____

_____

_____

_____

_____

_____

_____

_____

_____

_____

_____

_____

_____

_____

_____

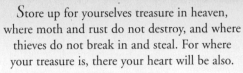

Store up for yourselves treasure in heaven,
where moth and rust do not destroy, and where
thieves do not break in and steal. For where
your treasure is, there your heart will be also.

Matthew 6:20–21

What could you be doing to "store up treasures in heaven?" Sharing about God with others? Learning to pray more deeply? Learning to sing or play an instrument that allows you to worship Him in a new way?

_____

_____

_____

_____

_____

_____

_____

_____

_____

_____

_____

_____

_____

_____

_____

_____

_____

_____

The precepts of the LORD are right,
giving joy to the heart. The commands of the
LORD are radiant, giving light to the eyes.

Psalm 19:8

*W*hat sets the Bible apart from all other books?

_____

_____

_____

_____

_____

_____

_____

_____

_____

_____

_____

_____

_____

_____

_____

_____

_____

_____

_____

_____

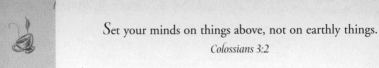

Set your minds on things above, not on earthly things.

Colossians 3:2

What activity can you begin today to help turn your
focus away from this temporary, trivial world and turn
it to our beloved Lord with whom we have all of eternity to
reap the benefits of our investment?

_____

_____

_____

_____

_____

_____

_____

_____

_____

_____

_____

_____

_____

_____

_____

_____

_____

_____

_____

_____

*T*he heavens are yours, and yours also the earth;
you founded the world and all that is in it.

Psalm 89:11

*D*o you enjoy the beauty of this world? It is a gift
from God!

_____

_____

_____

_____

_____

_____

_____

_____

_____

_____

_____

_____

_____

_____

_____

_____

_____

_____

_____

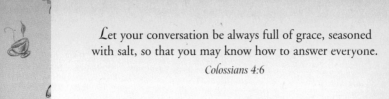

*L*et your conversation be always full of grace, seasoned with salt, so that you may know how to answer everyone.

Colossians 4:6

*A*re you ever tempted to take the quick opportunity to build yourself up by belittling someone else? Remember—your reputation will be protected and you will be honored if you can learn to speak kindly!

_____

_____

_____

_____

_____

_____

_____

_____

_____

_____

_____

_____

_____

_____

_____

_____

_____

_____

_____

*B*ut our citizenship is in heaven. And we eagerly await a
Savior from there, the Lord Jesus Christ.

Philippians 3:20

*A*re the things that mean the most to you the things that
will bring *eternal* joy and satisfaction?

_____

_____

_____

_____

_____

_____

_____

_____

_____

_____

_____

_____

_____

_____

_____

_____

_____

_____

_____

*T*here is a time to keep and a time to throw away.

Ecclesiastes 3:6b

*I*n the absence of the physical presence of a person, do you turn to God for comfort and help?

_____
_____
_____
_____
_____
_____
_____
_____
_____
_____
_____
_____
_____
_____
_____
_____
_____
_____
_____
_____
_____

> "*I* will be a Father to you, and you will be my
> sons and daughters," says the Lord Almighty.
>
> *2 Corinthians 6:18*

*H*ow near do you allow God to be? Do you consider
Him your Father . . . Lover . . . Friend?

_____

_____

_____

_____

_____

_____

_____

_____

_____

_____

_____

_____

_____

_____

_____

_____

_____

_____

_____

There is a time to tear and a time to mend,
a time to be silent and a time to speak.

Ecclesiastes 3:7

Have you ever made an excuse for "speaking your mind"—when it's an important issue others *need* to be informed about?

_____

_____

_____

_____

_____

_____

_____

_____

_____

_____

_____

_____

_____

_____

_____

_____

_____

_____

_____

*H*e was oppressed and afflicted, yet he did
not open his mouth; he was led like a lamb to
the slaughter, and as a sheep before her shearers
is silent, so he did not open his mouth.

Isaiah 53:7

*H*ow can we follow Christ's example of remaining silent
when wronged rather than "standing up for ourselves"?

_____

_____

_____

_____

_____

_____

_____

_____

_____

_____

_____

_____

_____

_____

_____

_____

_____

_____

_____

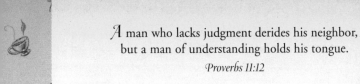

A man who lacks judgment derides his neighbor,
but a man of understanding holds his tongue.

Proverbs 11:12

*H*ow can exercising restraint help you to get what is
really important?

_____

_____

_____

_____

_____

_____

_____

_____

_____

_____

_____

_____

_____

_____

_____

_____

_____

_____

_____

Simon Peter and another disciple were following Jesus.
Because this disciple was known to the high priest,
he went with Jesus into the high priest's courtyard,
but Peter had to wait outside at the door.

John 18:15–16

Have you ever been recognized as a follower of Christ
even before discussing your faith? If we do it right, it
should show.

_____

_____

_____

_____

_____

_____

_____

_____

_____

_____

_____

_____

_____

_____

_____

_____

_____

_____

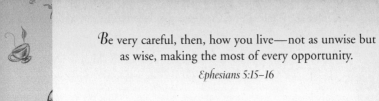

*B*e very careful, then, how you live—not as unwise but
as wise, making the most of every opportunity.

Ephesians 5:15–16

*D*o your actions confirm what your words sometimes
won't admit?

_____

_____

_____

_____

_____

_____

_____

_____

_____

_____

_____

_____

_____

_____

_____

_____

_____

_____

_____

*T*here is a time to love and a time to hate.

Ecclesiastes 3:8a

*W*hat small kindness have you given recently to demonstrate love to someone?

_____

_____

_____

_____

_____

_____

_____

_____

_____

_____

_____

_____

_____

_____

_____

_____

_____

_____

_____

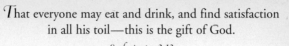

*T*hat everyone may eat and drink, and find satisfaction
in all his toil—this is the gift of God.

Ecclesiastes 3:13

*W*ould you get more satisfaction out of your chores by
looking at work as the plan that God has for our
existence on this earth?

_____

_____

_____

_____

_____

_____

_____

_____

_____

_____

_____

_____

_____

_____

_____

_____

_____

_____

We continually remember before our God and Father your work produced by faith, your labor prompted by love, and your endurance inspired by hope in our Lord Jesus Christ.

1 Thessalonians 1:3

*A*re you willing to be used to impart a legacy of Christ's love in the lives of those you encounter?

There is a time for war and a time for peace.

Ecclesiastes 3:8b

Will you choose to take time off from "work" to worship God and see what He's done for you? It's important to take time off to bring a measure of peace into your life.

_____

_____

_____

_____

_____

_____

_____

_____

_____

_____

_____

_____

_____

_____

_____

_____

_____

_____

_____

*C*onsecrate the fiftieth year and proclaim liberty throughout the land to all its inhabitants. It shall be a jubilee for you; each one of you is to return to his family property and each to his own clan.

Leviticus 25:10

*W*hat can we learn from this Old Testament tradition of Jubilee that can enrich our lives today?

_____

_____

_____

_____

_____

_____

_____

_____

_____

_____

_____

_____

_____

_____

_____

_____

_____

*I*t is for freedom that Christ has set us free.
Stand firm, then, and do not let yourselves
be burdened again by a yoke of slavery.

Galatians 5:1

*W*ill you set aside a time of "Jubilee" to cut back on commitments to refresh your spirit? You'll be ready to start a new phase of life with greater peace and contentment.

_____

_____

_____

_____

_____

_____

_____

_____

_____

_____

_____

_____

_____

_____

_____

_____

_____

_____

_____

The law of the LORD is perfect, reviving
the soul. The statutes of the LORD are
trustworthy, making wise the simple.

Psalm 19:7

*H*ave you ever heard a message and found you got
something different from it than someone else who
heard the same sermon? Did you simply hear the preacher
differently, or does the word of God have the power to
touch us in whatever our circumstances?

_____

_____

_____

_____

_____

_____

_____

_____

_____

_____

_____

_____

_____

_____

_____

_____

_____

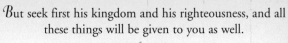

*B*ut seek first his kingdom and his righteousness, and all
these things will be given to you as well.

Matthew 6:33

*I*s your relationship with God a treasure to you?

_____

_____

_____

_____

_____

_____

_____

_____

_____

_____

_____

_____

_____

_____

_____

_____

_____

_____

*T*he fear of the LORD is pure, enduring forever. The ordinances of the LORD are sure and altogether righteous. They are more precious than gold, than much pure gold; they are sweeter than honey, than honey from the comb.

Psalm 19:9–10

*D*oes studying the Bible ever become routine? What steps can you take to revive your devotional time?

_____

_____

_____

_____

_____

_____

_____

_____

_____

_____

_____

_____

_____

_____

_____

_____

_____

_____

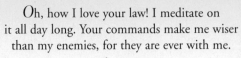

*O*h, how I love your law! I meditate on
it all day long. Your commands make me wiser
than my enemies, for they are ever with me.

Psalm 119:97–98

*A*re God's words the most precious words in your heart?

_____

_____

_____

_____

_____

_____

_____

_____

_____

_____

_____

_____

_____

_____

_____

_____

_____

_____

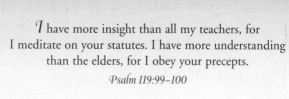

I have more insight than all my teachers, for
I meditate on your statutes. I have more understanding
than the elders, for I obey your precepts.

Psalm 119:99–100

*H*ave you acknowledged that there is a Master Plan that
the Creator has set in motion?

_____

_____

_____

_____

_____

_____

_____

_____

_____

_____

_____

_____

_____

_____

_____

_____

_____

_____

_____

I thank my God every time I remember you. In all my prayers for all of you, I always pray with joy because of your partnership in the gospel from the first day until now.

Philippians 1:3–5

*I*s there someone who you should thank God for right now? A friend or acquaintance who has made an impact in your life?

_____

_____

_____

_____

_____

_____

_____

_____

_____

_____

_____

_____

_____

_____

_____

_____

_____

_____

*T*hen Jesus told them, "You are going to have the light just a little while longer.... Put your trust in the light while you have it, so that you may become sons of light."

John 12:35–36

*H*ow do you react—when wrong has been done and "attention must be called to it?" When someone has been "getting away with" something and they *need* to be stopped?

_____

_____

_____

_____

_____

_____

_____

_____

_____

_____

_____

_____

_____

_____

_____

_____

_____

_____

*W*hoever obeys his command will come to no harm, and
the wise heart will know the proper time and procedure.
For there is a proper time and procedure for every matter.

Ecclesiastes 8:5–6

*D*o you think God is more concerned with the effect
giving has on us than what our actions mean to
someone else?

_____

_____

_____

_____

_____

_____

_____

_____

_____

_____

_____

_____

_____

_____

_____

_____

_____

_____

_____

Since no man knows the future,
who can tell him what is to come?

Ecclesiastes 8:7

Are you able to appreciate the beauty of the seasonal changes in your life?

_____

_____

_____

_____

_____

_____

_____

_____

_____

_____

_____

_____

_____

_____

_____

_____

_____

_____

_____

_____

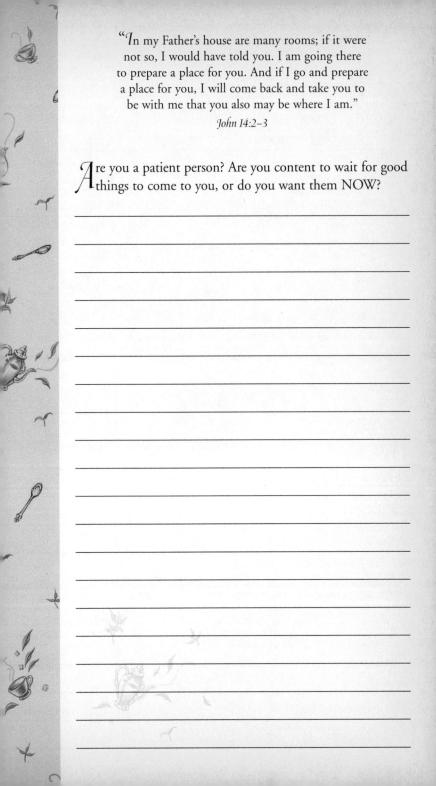

"*I*n my Father's house are many rooms; if it were not so, I would have told you. I am going there to prepare a place for you. And if I go and prepare a place for you, I will come back and take you to be with me that you also may be where I am."

John 14:2–3

*A*re you a patient person? Are you content to wait for good things to come to you, or do you want them NOW?

_____

_____

_____

_____

_____

_____

_____

_____

_____

_____

_____

_____

_____

_____

_____

_____

_____

_____

_____

_____

_____

I have chosen the way of truth;
I have set my heart on your laws.

Psalm 119:30

*A*re you striving to gain new insights into God's Word in
order to know Him more intimately?

*B*ut Joseph said to them, "Don't be afraid.
Am I in the place of God? You intended to harm
me, but God intended it for good to accomplish
what is now being done, the saving of many lives.

Genesis 50:19–20

*D*o you take care that your "body language" is telling
people what you want it to?

_____

_____

_____

_____

_____

_____

_____

_____

_____

_____

_____

_____

_____

_____

_____

_____

_____

_____

_____

*L*et no debt remain outstanding, except
the continuing debt to love one another, for he
who loves his fellowman has fulfilled the law.

Romans 13:8

*H*ave you ever stopped to think that, "You may be the
only Bible someone ever reads"?

_____

_____

_____

_____

_____

_____

_____

_____

_____

_____

_____

_____

_____

_____

_____

_____

_____

_____

_____

_____

O LORD, my strength and my fortress,
my refuge in time of distress.
Jeremiah 16:19

*D*o you find yourself with more tasks than time on
certain days? Rather than cut your time with the Lord
short, how about spending extra time praying for His
strength and provision?

_____

_____

_____

_____

_____

_____

_____

_____

_____

_____

_____

_____

_____

_____

_____

_____

_____

_____

*I*n his love and mercy he redeemed them;
he lifted them up and carried them all the days of old.

Isaiah 63:9

*W*inter is a time of rest. A time to live off the provisions that were stored up from the harvest. Are you properly preparing and nurturing so you'll be ready for the Winter season of life?

_____

_____

_____

_____

_____

_____

_____

_____

_____

_____

_____

_____

_____

_____

_____

_____

_____

_____

_____

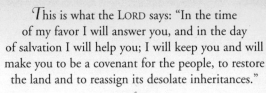

*T*his is what the LORD says: "In the time
of my favor I will answer you, and in the day
of salvation I will help you; I will keep you and will
make you to be a covenant for the people, to restore
the land and to reassign its desolate inheritances."

Isaiah 49:8

*I*s your devotional time with the Lord a special, celebrated
time? Can you approach it with more excitement?

_____

_____

_____

_____

_____

_____

_____

_____

_____

_____

_____

_____

_____

_____

_____

_____

_____

_____

"*For* your Father knows what you need
before you ask him."

Matthew 6:8

*A*ren't you thankful God is not limited by our requests?
Does this affect how you pray? What you pray for?

_____

_____

_____

_____

_____

_____

_____

_____

_____

_____

_____

_____

_____

_____

_____

_____

_____

_____

_____

*F*or the revelation awaits an appointed time; it speaks of the end and will not prove false. Though it linger, wait for it; it will certainly come and will not delay.

Habakkuk 2:3

*C*an time be banked or hoarded? What can you do to make the most of the time you *do* have?

_____

_____

_____

_____

_____

_____

_____

_____

_____

_____

_____

_____

_____

_____

_____

_____

_____

_____

_____

_____

*T*he LORD your God is with you, he is mighty to save.
He will take great delight in you, he will quiet you
with his love, he will rejoice over you with singing.

Zephaniah 3:17

*T*he next time you find yourself talking too much (or
commenting too quickly) ask yourself, "Is it true? Is it
kind? Is it necessary?"

_____

_____

_____

_____

_____

_____

_____

_____

_____

_____

_____

_____

_____

_____

_____

_____

_____

_____

Cast all your anxiety on him because he cares for you.
1 Peter 5:7

What are your fears? Are you anxious about the
future—for yourself? your husband? your children?
your grandchildren?

_____

_____

_____

_____

_____

_____

_____

_____

_____

_____

_____

_____

_____

_____

_____

_____

_____

_____

_____

*Encourage one another daily, as long as it is called Today,
so that none of you may be hardened by sin's deceitfulness.*

Hebrews 3:13

*Wouldn't you rather be known for your "graciousness"
than for your bluntness? How do others describe you?*

_____

_____

_____

_____

_____

_____

_____

_____

_____

_____

_____

_____

_____

_____

_____

_____

_____

_____

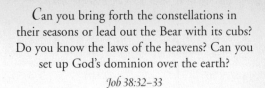

*C*an you bring forth the constellations in
their seasons or lead out the Bear with its cubs?
Do you know the laws of the heavens? Can you
set up God's dominion over the earth?

Job 38:32–33

*W*hat an amazing God we have! Isn't it humbling to
know that we can come before Him and have a
personal relationship with God?

_____

_____

_____

_____

_____

_____

_____

_____

_____

_____

_____

_____

_____

_____

_____

_____

_____

_____

_____

I thank my God every time I remember you. In all my prayers for all of you, I always pray with joy because of your partnership in the gospel from the first day until now.

Philippians 1:3–5

*D*id you know that the Bible has a great deal to say about the tongue? Can you find where Scripture tells about the dangers of talking too much, of lying, gossiping and being unkind?

_____

_____

_____

_____

_____

_____

_____

_____

_____

_____

_____

_____

_____

_____

_____

_____

_____

_____

*H*e who began a good work in you will carry it on
to completion until the day of Christ Jesus.

Philippians 1:6

*W*hen sharing the word of God within your family, how
can you make sure the rocks and weeds have been
removed, that you've supplied plenty of water and protected
them from influences that will snatch the seed away?

_____

_____

_____

_____

_____

_____

_____

_____

_____

_____

_____

_____

_____

_____

_____

_____

_____

_____

_____

_____

_____

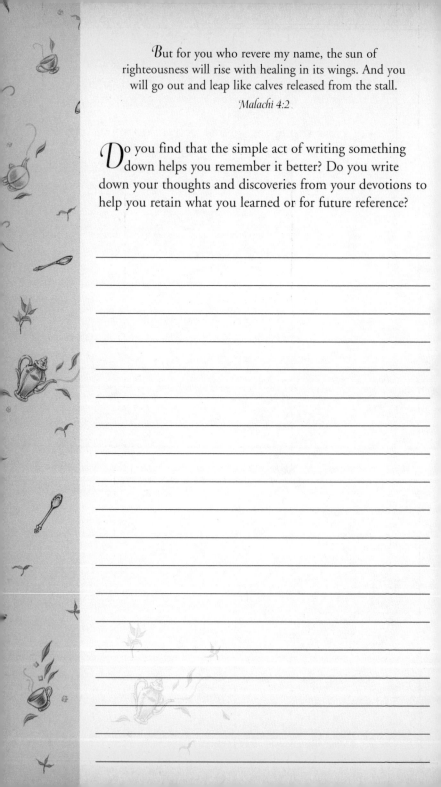

*B*ut for you who revere my name, the sun of
righteousness will rise with healing in its wings. And you
will go out and leap like calves released from the stall.

Malachi 4:2

*D*o you find that the simple act of writing something
down helps you remember it better? Do you write
down your thoughts and discoveries from your devotions to
help you retain what you learned or for future reference?

_____

_____

_____

_____

_____

_____

_____

_____

_____

_____

_____

_____

_____

_____

_____

_____

_____

_____

No one knows about that day or hour, not even the angels in heaven, nor the Son, but only the Father. Be on guard! Be alert! You do not know when that time will come.

Mark 13:32–33

When we look at the example we have in Jesus Christ and then take a look at ourselves, do we even have the time to look at the shortcomings of others?

_____

_____

_____

_____

_____

_____

_____

_____

_____

_____

_____

_____

_____

_____

_____

_____

_____

_____

_____

*A*t that time they will see the Son of Man coming
in a cloud with power and great glory. When these
things begin to take place, stand up and lift up your
heads, because your redemption is drawing near.

Luke 21:27–28

*H*ave you ever justified questionable choices in music,
books or movies by saying that you need to be aware
of where the culture is going? Do you see any danger in
that justification?

_____

_____

_____

_____

_____

_____

_____

_____

_____

_____

_____

_____

_____

_____

_____

_____

_____

_____

The heavens declare the glory of God;
the skies proclaim the work of his hands.

Psalm 19:1

*W*hat have you learned about God through observing
nature? What does it "say" about God to you?

_____

_____

_____

_____

_____

_____

_____

_____

_____

_____

_____

_____

_____

_____

_____

_____

_____

_____

_____

Yet a time is coming and has now come when the true worshipers will worship the Father in spirit and truth, for they are the kind of worshipers the Father seeks.

John 4:23

Does it encourage you to know that God will always meet your needs, even when you ask for only what you think you want?

_____

_____

_____

_____

_____

_____

_____

_____

_____

_____

_____

_____

_____

_____

_____

_____

_____

_____

_____

My soul is consumed with longing for your laws at all
times.

Psalm 119:20

*I*s your soul thriving? Is the Bible growing more and more
precious to you?

_____

_____

_____

_____

_____

_____

_____

_____

_____

_____

_____

_____

_____

_____

_____

_____

_____

_____

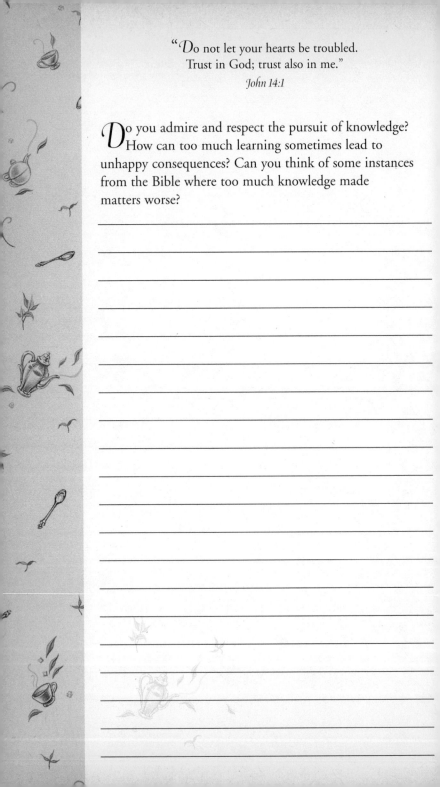

"*D*o not let your hearts be troubled.
Trust in God; trust also in me."

John 14:1

*D*o you admire and respect the pursuit of knowledge?
How can too much learning sometimes lead to
unhappy consequences? Can you think of some instances
from the Bible where too much knowledge made
matters worse?

_____

_____

_____

_____

_____

_____

_____

_____

_____

_____

_____

_____

_____

_____

_____

_____

_____

_____

Give thanks to the LORD, for he is good.
His love endures forever.

Psalm 136:1

Did you know God will honor you for giving extra even to your enemies?

_____

_____

_____

_____

_____

_____

_____

_____

_____

_____

_____

_____

_____

_____

_____

_____

_____

_____

_____

_____

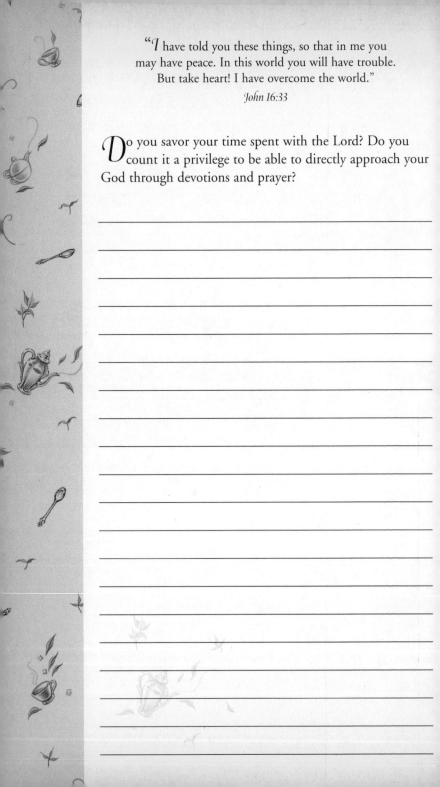

"*I* have told you these things, so that in me you
may have peace. In this world you will have trouble.
But take heart! I have overcome the world."

John 16:33

*D*o you savor your time spent with the Lord? Do you
count it a privilege to be able to directly approach your
God through devotions and prayer?

He who guards his mouth and
his tongue keeps himself from calamity.

Proverbs 21:23

*D*o you evaluate your comments before making them?

_____

_____

_____

_____

_____

_____

_____

_____

_____

_____

_____

_____

_____

_____

_____

_____

_____

_____

_____

_____

I know, O LORD, that a man's life is not his own;
it is not for man to direct his steps.

Jeremiah 10:23

*D*o you trust God to always provide just what you need at the right time?

_____

_____

_____

_____

_____

_____

_____

_____

_____

_____

_____

_____

_____

_____

_____

_____

_____

_____

_____

_____

*E*very day [the believers] continued to meet together
in the temple courts. They broke bread in their homes
and ate together with glad and sincere hearts, praising
God and enjoying the favor of all the people.

Acts 2:46–47

*W*hat aspect(s) of your job can you thank God
for today?

_____

_____

_____

_____

_____

_____

_____

_____

_____

_____

_____

_____

_____

_____

_____

_____

_____

_____

_____

Even the stork in the sky knows her appointed seasons, and the dove, the swift and the thrush observe the time of their migration. But my people do not know the requirements of the LORD.

Jeremiah 8:7

*H*ow much of your time is spent trying to please others instead of pleasing God?

_____

_____

_____

_____

_____

_____

_____

_____

_____

_____

_____

_____

_____

_____

_____

_____

_____

_____

We do not know what we ought to pray for,
but the Spirit himself intercedes for us with groans that
words cannot express. And he who searches our hearts
knows the mind of the Spirit, because the Spirit intercedes
for the saints in accordance with God's will.

Romans 8:26–27

*D*id you know the Bible speaks more about remaining silent when wronged than it does about standing up for ourselves?

_____

_____

_____

_____

_____

_____

_____

_____

_____

_____

_____

_____

_____

_____

_____

_____

I know, O LORD, that a man's life is not his own;
it is not for man to direct his steps.

Jeremiah 10:23

*D*o you believe that God really can work wonders when
we are faithful to do our part?

_____

_____

_____

_____

_____

_____

_____

_____

_____

_____

_____

_____

_____

_____

_____

_____

_____

_____

_____

_____

Since ancient times no one has heard, no ear has
perceived, no eye has seen any God besides you,
who acts on behalf of those who wait for him.

Isaiah 64:4

Who do you consider to be your best friend? Did you
know you can have confidence that the hands of
God will hold you close in ways that no earthly friend
ever could?

_____

_____

_____

_____

_____

_____

_____

_____

_____

_____

_____

_____

_____

_____

_____

_____

_____

_____

*T*herefore judge nothing before the appointed time; wait till the Lord comes. He will bring to light what is hidden in darkness and will expose the motives of men's hearts. At that time each will receive his praise from God.

1 Corinthians 4:5

*I*s it your goal to *always* show that you are a follower of Christ—or only when someone's watching?

_____

_____

_____

_____

_____

_____

_____

_____

_____

_____

_____

_____

_____

_____

_____

_____

_____

_____

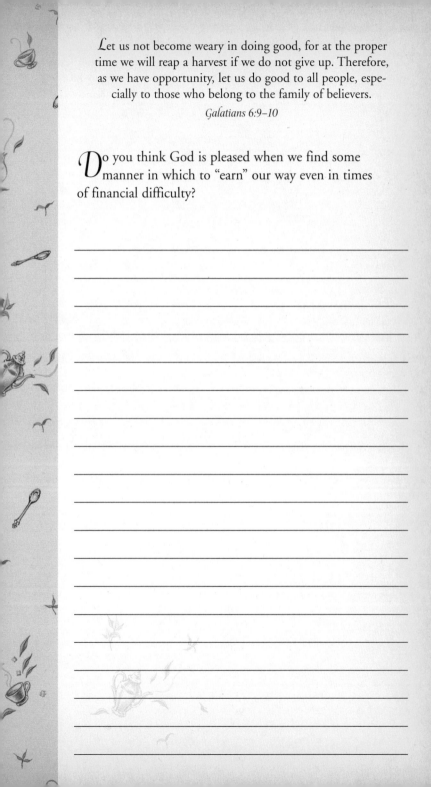

*L*et us not become weary in doing good, for at the proper time we will reap a harvest if we do not give up. Therefore, as we have opportunity, let us do good to all people, especially to those who belong to the family of believers.

Galatians 6:9–10

*D*o you think God is pleased when we find some manner in which to "earn" our way even in times of financial difficulty?

_____

_____

_____

_____

_____

_____

_____

_____

_____

_____

_____

_____

_____

_____

_____

_____

_____

_____

And pray in the Spirit on all occasions with all kinds of prayers and requests. With this in mind, be alert and always keep on praying for all the saints.

Ephesians 6:18

*H*ave you made a commitment to bring Christ honor and glory rather than dishonor?

_____

_____

_____

_____

_____

_____

_____

_____

_____

_____

_____

_____

_____

_____

_____

_____

_____

_____

I have kept my feet from every evil path so that
I might obey your word. I have not departed from
your laws, for you yourself have taught me.

Psalm 119:101–102

*H*ow can you lead others up if you've allowed yourself to
be stuck in the mire of the world below?

_____

_____

_____

_____

_____

_____

_____

_____

_____

_____

_____

_____

_____

_____

_____

_____

_____

_____

_____

Being confident of this, that he
who began a good work in you will carry it on
to completion until the day of Christ Jesus.

Philippians 1:6

Do your actions speak louder than your words—
hopefully, to let people know you're a follower of
Christ, even without saying a word?

_____

_____

_____

_____

_____

_____

_____

_____

_____

_____

_____

_____

_____

_____

_____

_____

_____

_____

_____

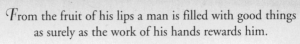

*F*rom the fruit of his lips a man is filled with good things
as surely as the work of his hands rewards him.

Proverbs 12:14

*W*ho do you most admire or enjoy being around?
Is it someone who can be described as "able to put
someone in her place, using sarcastic, biting humor"
or as "kind, gracious, never has a bad thing to say
about anyone"?

_____

_____

_____

_____

_____

_____

_____

_____

_____

_____

_____

_____

_____

_____

_____

_____

_____

_____

But join with me in suffering for the gospel,
by the power of God, who has saved us and called us
to a holy life—not because of anything we have done
but because of his own purpose and grace.

2 Timothy 1:8–9

*W*hen was the last time you were able to be alone with
God? Would it be possible to leave behind family,
friends and commitments for a short period of time to
strengthen your relationship with God?

_____

_____

_____

_____

_____

_____

_____

_____

_____

_____

_____

_____

_____

_____

_____

_____

_____

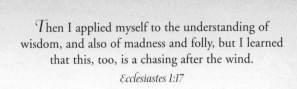

*T*hen I applied myself to the understanding of
wisdom, and also of madness and folly, but I learned
that this, too, is a chasing after the wind.

Ecclesiastes 1:17

*H*ow much effort do you put into selecting the right
books and videos for your children? Do you apply that
same wisdom to your own choices—in movies and
television shows, books and music?

_____

_____

_____

_____

_____

_____

_____

_____

_____

_____

_____

_____

_____

_____

_____

_____

_____

_____

See! The winter is past; the rains are over and gone. Flowers appear on the earth; the season of singing has come, the cooing of doves is heard in our land.

Song of Songs 2:11–12

Are you amazed at God's control over the change of seasons?

_____

_____

_____

_____

_____

_____

_____

_____

_____

_____

_____

_____

_____

_____

_____

_____

_____

_____

*£et us then approach the throne of grace
with confidence, so that we may receive mercy
and find grace to help us in our time of need.*

Hebrews 4:16

Do you need a reminder to take time off to bring a measure of peace into your hectic life? Are you so busy balancing responsibilities of family, friends and work that you've neglected your own quiet time with God?

_____

_____

_____

_____

_____

_____

_____

_____

_____

_____

_____

_____

_____

_____

_____

_____

Sow your seed in the morning, and at evening let not your hands be idle, for you do not know which will succeed.

Ecclesiastes 11:6

*D*o you ever hesitate to witness because the opportunity seems too obscure or impossible?

_____

_____

_____

_____

_____

_____

_____

_____

_____

_____

_____

_____

_____

_____

_____

_____

_____

_____

*N*o discipline seems pleasant at the time, but painful.
Later on, however, it produces a harvest of righteousness
and peace for those who have been trained by it.

Hebrews 12:11

*T*he next time you have "one of those days" when
nothing seems to be going right, can you stop and ask
the Lord what He might be trying to teach you in your
present circumstances?

_____

_____

_____

_____

_____

_____

_____

_____

_____

_____

_____

_____

_____

_____

_____

_____

_____

_____

_____

*T*herefore, prepare your minds for action; be
self-controlled; set your hope fully on the grace
to be given you when Jesus Christ is revealed.

1 Peter 1:13

*A*re you a friend who keeps her promises? Do you
ever take it for granted that God will always keep
His promises?

_____

_____

_____

_____

_____

_____

_____

_____

_____

_____

_____

_____

_____

_____

_____

_____

_____

_____

_____

*H*umble yourselves, therefore, under God's mighty
hand, that he may lift you up in due time.

1 Peter 5:6

*D*o you consider yourself a humble person? How do you
"humble yourself?"

_____

_____

_____

_____

_____

_____

_____

_____

_____

_____

_____

_____

_____

_____

_____

_____

_____

_____

_____

_____

"At that time I will gather you; at that time I will bring you home. I will give you honor and praise among all the peoples of the earth when I restore your fortunes before your very eyes," says the LORD.

Zephaniah 3:20

Are you valuable to God because of your wealth or status or religion?

_____

_____

_____

_____

_____

_____

_____

_____

_____

_____

_____

_____

_____

_____

_____

_____

_____

_____

_____

"*If* you follow my decrees and are careful to obey my commands, I will send you rain in its season, and the ground will yield its crops and the trees of the field their fruit."

Leviticus 26:3–4

*C*an you thank God for His provisions in nature?

_____

_____

_____

_____

_____

_____

_____

_____

_____

_____

_____

_____

_____

_____

_____

_____

_____

_____

_____

_____

*P*reach the Word; be prepared in season and
out of season; correct, rebuke and encourage—
with great patience and careful instruction.

2 Timothy 4:2

*I*s the only right way *your* way? How can you become
more flexible and "giving"—with your husband? parents?
children? co-workers?

_____

_____

_____

_____

_____

_____

_____

_____

_____

_____

_____

_____

_____

_____

_____

_____

_____

_____

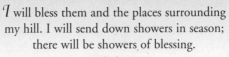

I will bless them and the places surrounding
my hill. I will send down showers in season;
there will be showers of blessing.

Ezekiel 34:26

*D*o you ever stop to think how much we take God's
control and timing of nature for granted?

_____

_____

_____

_____

_____

_____

_____

_____

_____

_____

_____

_____

_____

_____

_____

_____

_____

_____

_____

O LORD, you have searched me and
you know me. You know when I sit and when
I rise; you perceive my thoughts from afar.

Psalm 139:1–2

With whom do you spend the largest portion of your day? Have you stopped to comprehend what it means to have God with you *constantly*?

_____

_____

_____

_____

_____

_____

_____

_____

_____

_____

_____

_____

_____

_____

_____

_____

_____

_____

_____

*F*orgetting what is behind and straining toward what is
ahead, I press on toward the goal to win the prize for which
God has called me heavenward in Christ Jesus.

Philippians 3:13–14

*H*ave you ever found it was necessary to endure extremes
in your life in order to find the wealth you have inside?

_____

_____

_____

_____

_____

_____

_____

_____

_____

_____

_____

_____

_____

_____

_____

_____

_____

_____

_____

*A*nd we rejoice in the hope of the glory of God.
Not only so, but we also rejoice in our sufferings,
because we know that suffering produces perseverance;
perseverance, character; and character, hope.

Romans 5:2–4

*W*hat ways can you find to make *eternal* investments?

_____

_____

_____

_____

_____

_____

_____

_____

_____

_____

_____

_____

_____

_____

_____

_____

_____

_____

_____

_____